THE WONDER OF SHARKS

THE WONDER OF SHARKS

FOG
CITY

PRESS

Published by Fog City Press,
a division of Weldon Owen Inc.
415 Jackson Street
San Francisco, CA 94111 USA

www.weldonowen.com

weldon**owen**
President, CEO Terry Newell
VP, Publisher Roger Shaw
Associate Publisher Mariah Bear
Project Editor Bridget Fitzgerald
Creative Director Kelly Booth
Art Director Meghan Hildebrand
Production Director Chris Hemesath
Associate Production Director Michelle Duggan
Consultant Dr. William White

Library of Congress Control Number on file with the publisher.

ISBN 13: 978-1-61628-790-0
ISBN 10: 1-61628-790-X

10 9 8 7 6 5 4 3 2

2015 2016

Printed in China.

Sharks are amazing creatures. Most sharks are fierce fish that hunt other sea creatures. They have very sharp teeth for biting food. But you should not be afraid of them. As long as you keep out of their way, sharks will leave you alone.

Sharks live in oceans all over the world. But many people have never seen one. Much of the time, sharks are far out to sea and deep underwater. Sharks can be many beautiful shapes and sizes. Which one is your favorite?

A shark has long, pointed fins that stick out of its body. The fin on its back can sometimes poke out of the water.

Great White Shark

Whaler Shark

Lemon Sharks

Fun Fact
There are over 500 different species of sharks.

Grey Reef Shark

Fun Fact

Like us, sharks have a heart with four chambers.

Grey Reef Shark

Blacktip Reef Shark

Sharks swim by beating their tails from side to side. The side fins help them to steer.

Fun Fact

The fastest sharks can swim up to 43 mph (70 kph)!

Great White Shark

Great White Shark

Large sharks can swim very fast and jump out of the water when hunting near the surface.

Whaler Shark

Sharks breathe underwater by passing water over featherly structures inside their heads called gills.

Sand Tiger Shark

Fun Fact

Sharks don't have bones! They have cartilage instead.

Caribbean Reef Sharks

Blacktip Reef Shark

Fun Fact

Sharks don't chew their food, they swallow it whole.

Great White Shark

Most sharks are meat-eaters. They eat other animals such as fish, dolphins, squid, and seals.

Whaler Shark

Catshark

Many sharks have eyes that point up and forward. They cannot see much of what is happening beneath them.

Sand Tiger Shark

Fun Fact

Sharks can see behind them as well as in front.

Lemon Shark

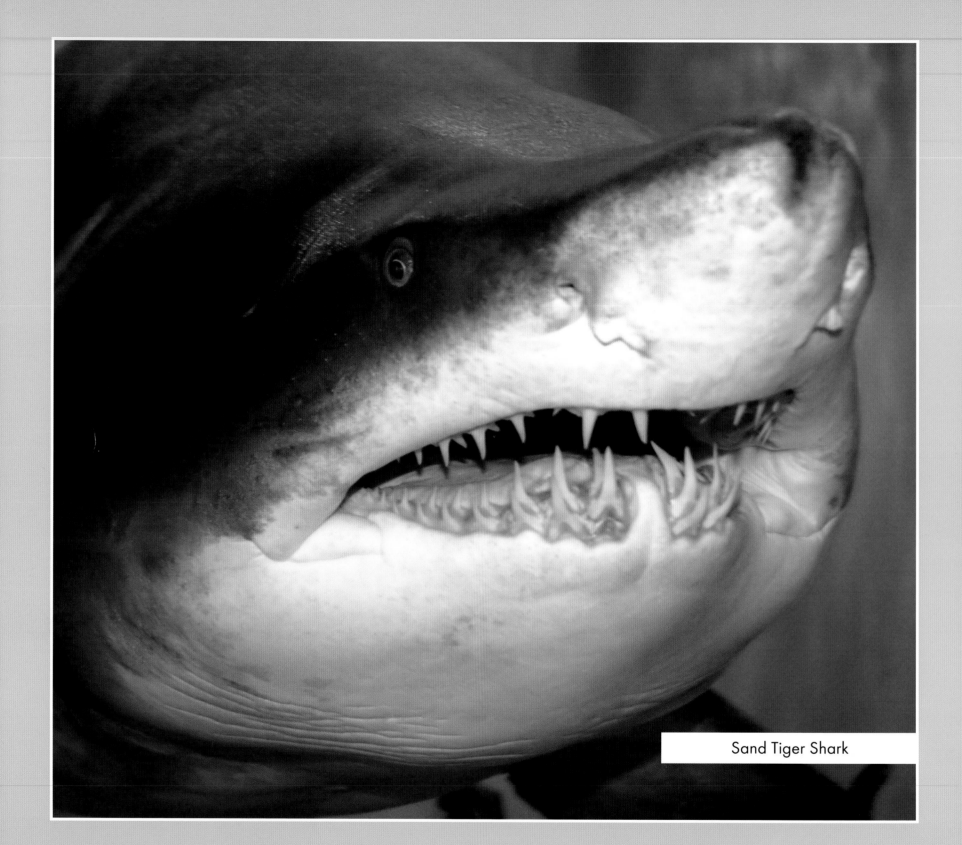

Sand Tiger Shark

Sharks have wide mouths full of pointed teeth lined up in two or three rows, so every bite counts!

Fun Fact

A shark's jaws are twice as powerful as a lion's.

Sand Tiger Shark

Fun Fact
Great Whites are the most dangerous sharks.

Great White Shark

Great White Shark

Great White Shark

A shark's sensory system can detect electricity coming from the bodies of other animals. This helps them find food.

Coral reefs are feeding grounds for many sharks.

Sand Tiger Shark

Caribbean Reef Shark

Grey Reef Shark

Fun Fact

Sharks can be picky eaters—like a lot of people!

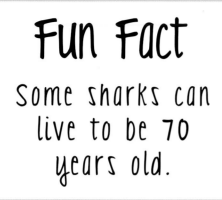

Fun Fact

Some sharks can live to be 70 years old.

Lemon Shark

Grey Whaler Shark

Big sharks live in deep water. Their skin colors can make them hard to see in the water.

Fun Fact

A group of sharks is known as a school of sharks!

School of Sharks

Tasseled Wobbegong Shark

Sharks do not need bright light to find food. They often hunt at night or in deep, dark water.

Scalloped Hammerhead Sharks

Great Hammerhead Shark

This shark looks a bit different! Can you guess where the hammerhead shark gets its name?

Fun Fact

Hammerheads have the best sense of smell.

Scalloped Hammerhead Shark

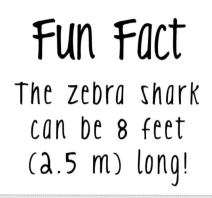

Fun Fact

The zebra shark can be 8 feet (2.5 m) long!

Zebra Shark

Swellshark

The swellshark is only 39 inches (100 cm) long, but grows to twice its size to protect itself from predators!

Blacktip Reef Shark

Caribbean Reef Shark

Sharks search for food everywhere they go. These sharks are exploring around a shipwreck.

34

Fun Fact

Some kinds of sharks eat smaller sharks!

Caribbean Reef Shark

Nurse Shark

Epaulette Shark

Some sharks look for food on the seabed. They use their fleshy whiskers, called barbels, to find food in the sand.

Fun Fact

Angel sharks eat
fish, mollusks,
and crustaceans.

Angel Shark

Fun Fact

Leopard sharks
eat shrimp, crabs,
and clams.

Baby Leopard Shark

Bamboo Shark

These sharks have patterned skin to blend in with their surroundings.

Leopard Shark

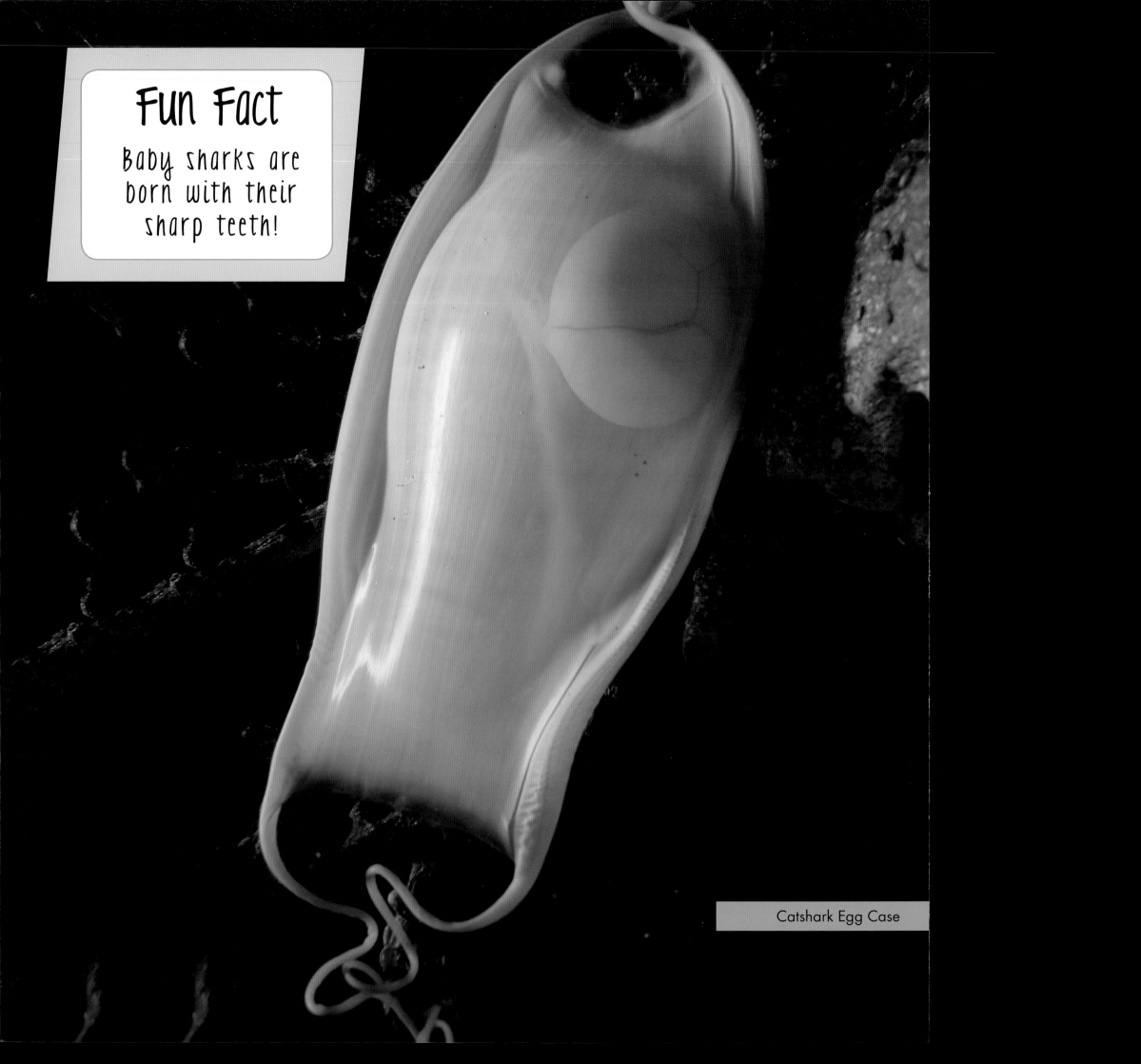

Fun Fact

Baby sharks are born with their sharp teeth!

Catshark Egg Case

Catshark Egg Cases

Many baby sharks are born live. Others hatch from egg cases like these. An egg case is called a mermaid's purse.

Some small fish, such as remora, follow sharks around. These fish nibble on the sharks' skin, cleaning it and eating any leftover food.

Whale Shark and Remoras

Bull Shark and Remoras

Fun Fact
Remoras are sometimes called suckerfish.

Grey Reef Sharks and Remoras

Tiger Shark

Expert divers can get very close to sharks to study them.

Fun Fact

Sharks don't get cavities, and they can regrow teeth.

Fun Fact

Sharks do not sleep like us—they just rest.

Sandbar Shark

Sand Tiger Shark

Fish and Sharks

A good place to see a shark is at an aquarium, which is a kind of underwater zoo. Have you ever seen a shark?

Lemon Sharks

Key t=top; b=bottom; DT=Dreamstime; iSP=iStockphoto;
CB=Corbis; SS=Shutterstock

2, 5 iSP; 7, 8, 9, 10, 11t SS; 11b DT; 12 iSP; 13 SS; 14t DT; 14b, 15, 16 SS; 17t DT; 17b iSP; 18t SS; 18b DT; 19, 20 SS; 21 DT; 22 CB; 23t iSP; 23b CB; 24t DT; 24b, 25, 26, 27 SS; 28 DT; 29, 30t SS; 30b, 31 iSP; 32, 33t SS; 33b DT; 34, 35, 36t SS; 36b iSP; 37 DT; 38 SS; 39t DT; 39b SS; 40 iSP; 41 SS; 42t DT; 42b, 43, 44, 45 SS; 46 iSP; 47 DT; 48 SS.